Donated by the Ferson
Creek PTO in memory of
Debra Johnson, Nathan's
mother. March, 2003

B252 © APCo

D1377000

I want to be a Nurse

Other titles in this series:

I want to be a Cowboy
I want to be a Firefighter
I want to be a Pilot
I want to be a Police Officer
I want to be a Vet
I want to be a Doctor
I want to be a Teacher
I want to be a Truck Driver

I WANT TO BE A

Nurse

DAN LIEBMAN

FIREFLY BOOKS

A FIREFLY BOOK

Published by Firefly Books Ltd. 2001

Copyright © 2001 Firefly Books Ltd.

All rights reserved. No part of this publication may be reproduced, stored in a retrieval system or transmitted in any form or by any means, electronic, mechanical, photocopying, recording or otherwise, without the prior written permission of the Publisher.

First Printing

Canadian Cataloguing in Publication Data

Liebman, Daniel
  I want to be a nurse

ISBN 1-55209-568-1 (bound)   ISBN 1-55209-566-5 (pbk.)

1. Nurses – Juvenile literature.   I. Title

RT82.L545 2001   j610.73'06'9   C00-932619-7

Published in Canada in 2001 by
Firefly Books Ltd.
3680 Victoria Park Avenue
Willowdale, Ontario, Canada
M2H 3K1

U.S. Cataloging-in-Publication Data
(Library of Congress Standards)

Liebman, Daniel
  I want to be a nurse / Dan Liebman. —1st ed.

[24] p. : col. ill. ; 20 cm. –(I want to be)
Summary : Photos and easy-to-read text
describe the job of a nurse.
ISBN 1-55209-566-5 (bound)
ISBN 1-55209-568-1 (pbk.)
1. Nursing – Vocational guidance. 2. Occupations
I. Title. II. Series
610.73069 21   2001   AC   CIP

Published in the United States in 2001 by
Firefly Books (U.S.) Inc.
P.O. Box 1338, Ellicott Station
Buffalo, New York, USA
14205

Photo Credits

© First Light/Simon Murrel, front cover
© First Light/Melanie Carr, page 15
© Al Harvey, page 22
© First Light/Rob Lewine, page 23
© Julian Calder/Stone, page 5
© David Hanover/Stone, page 6
© Charles Thatcher/Stone, page 8
© Elie Bernager/Stone, page 11
© Jonathan Selig/Stone, pages 12-13

© Stone, page 14
© Berwyn MRI Center/David Joel/Stone, pages 18-19
© David Joel/Stone, pages 18-19
© CORBIS/Jennie Woodcock, page 7
© CORBIS/Jacques M. Chenet, page 16
© CORBIS/Ed Young, page 17
© CORBIS/Stephanie Maze, pages 20-21
© CORBIS/Ted Spiegel, page 24
© Photodisc, pages 9, 10, back cover

Design by Interrobang Graphic Design Inc.
Printed and bound in Canada by Friesens, Altona, Manitoba

The Publisher acknowledges the financial support of the Government of Canada through the Book Publishing Industry Development Program for its publishing activities.

This nurse enjoys her job. She cares for the sick and helps people stay well.

Many nurses work in a hospital. Doctors and nurses work closely together.

A nurse welcomes a new patient and his friends.

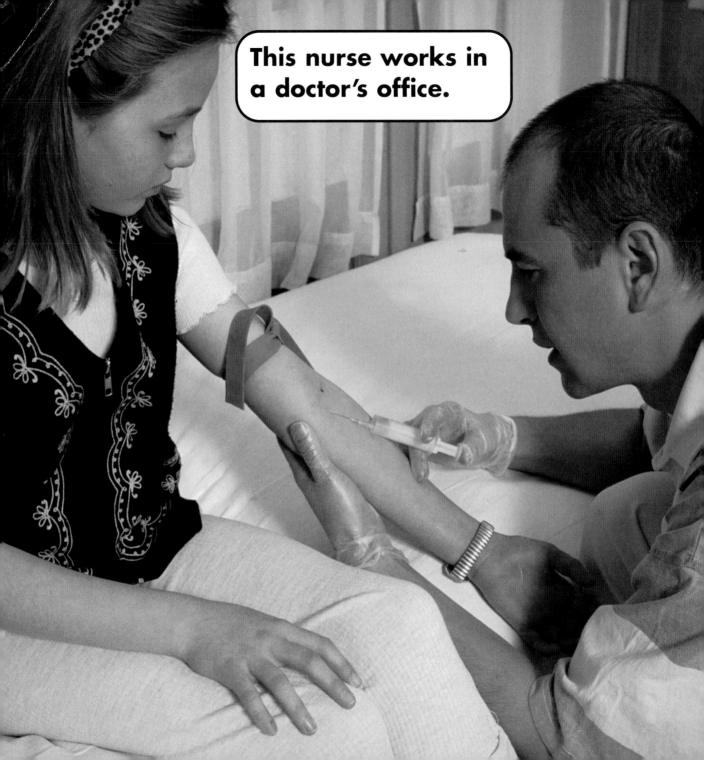

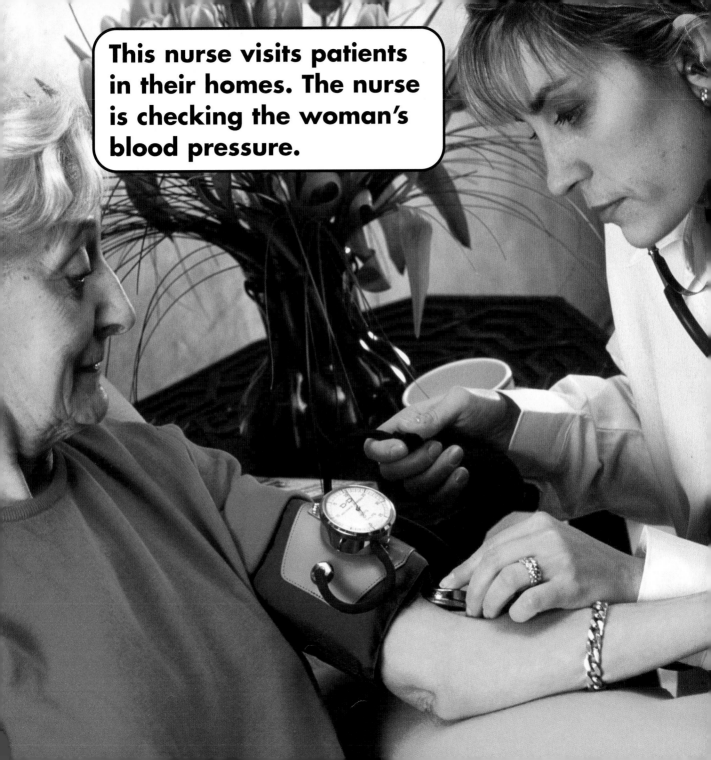

This nurse visits patients in their homes. The nurse is checking the woman's blood pressure.

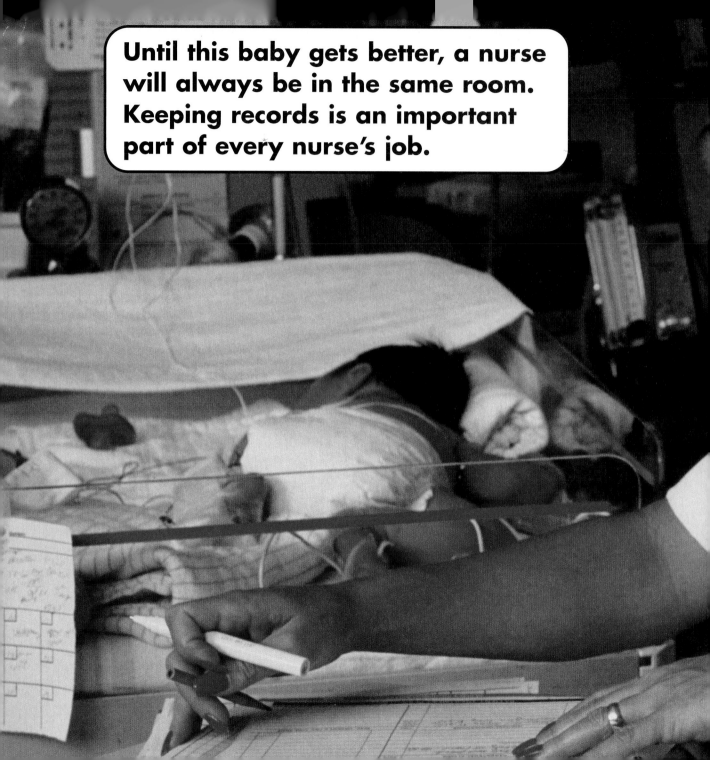

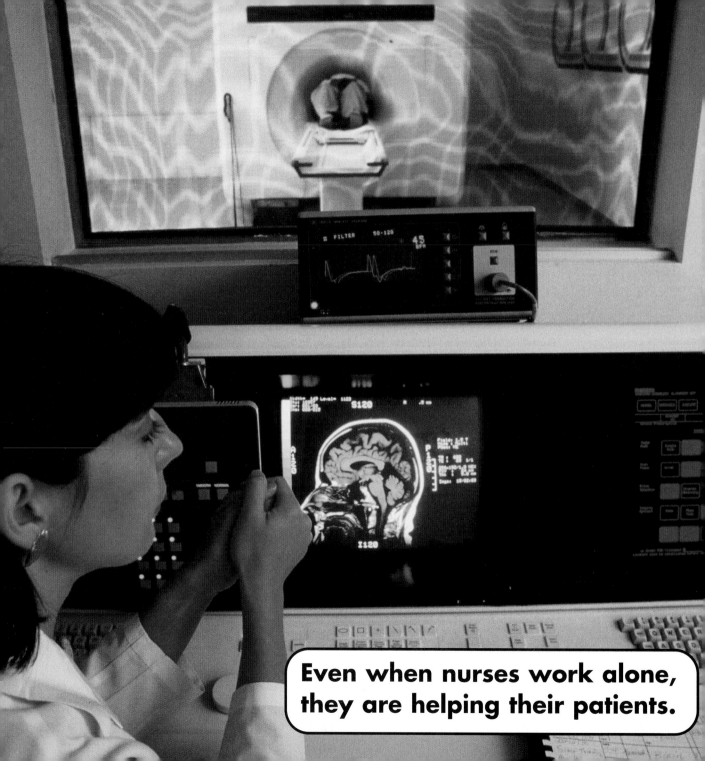

Even when nurses work alone, they are helping their patients.

Nurses learn to use special machines to check their patients' health.

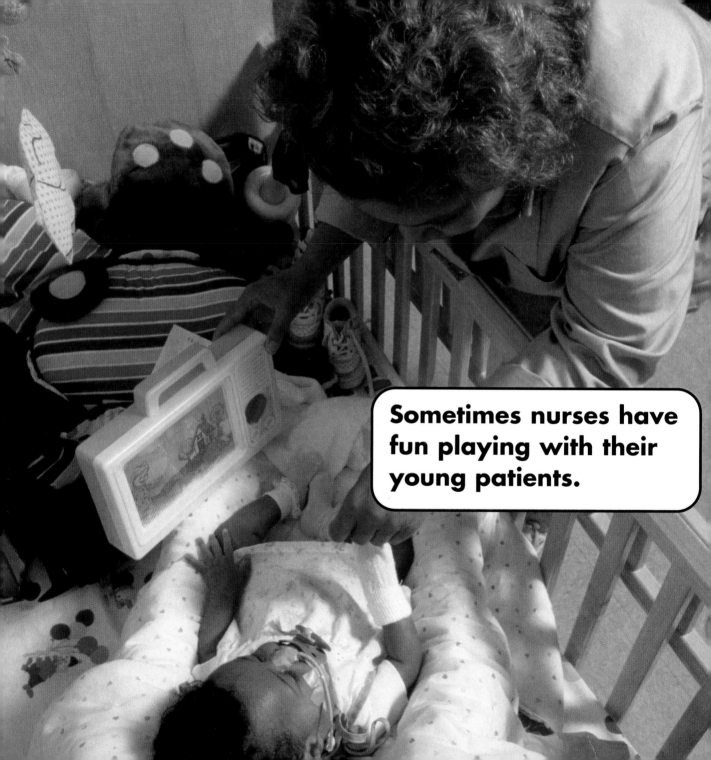

Sometimes nurses have fun playing with their young patients.

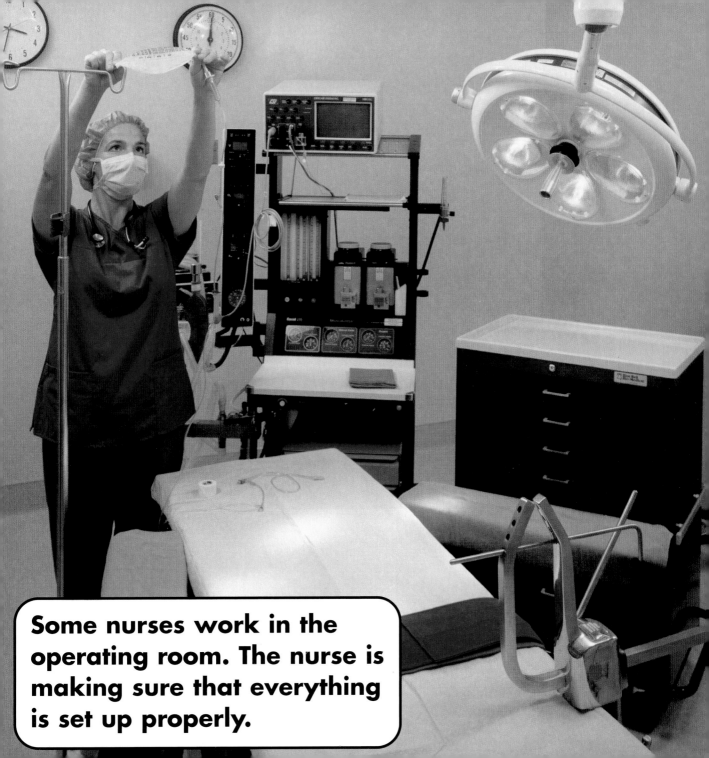

Some nurses work in the operating room. The nurse is making sure that everything is set up properly.

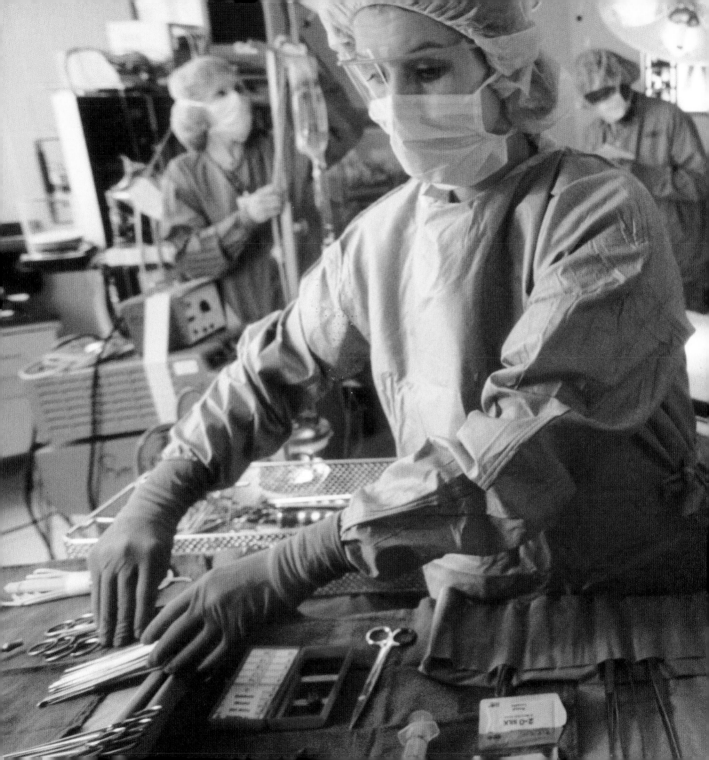

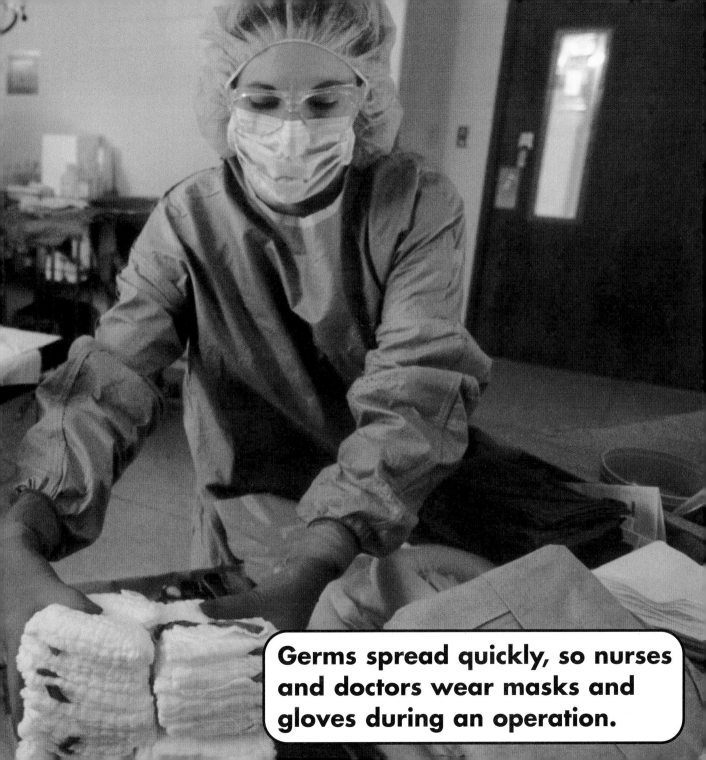

Germs spread quickly, so nurses and doctors wear masks and gloves during an operation.

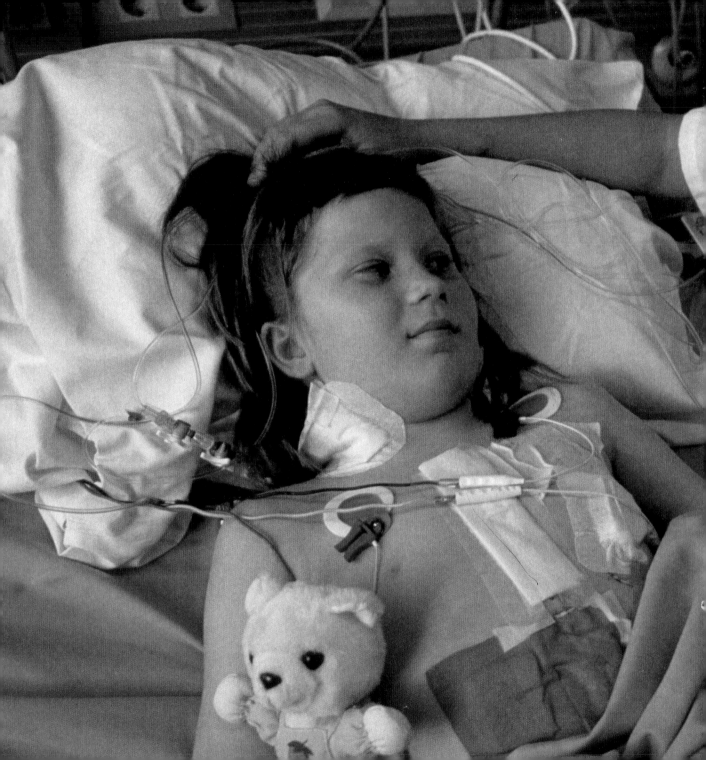

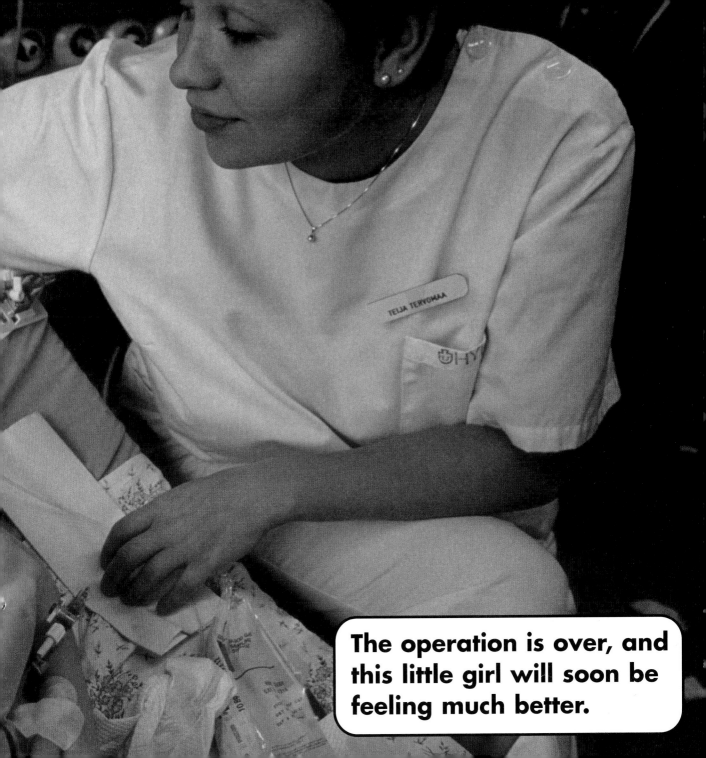

The operation is over, and this little girl will soon be feeling much better.

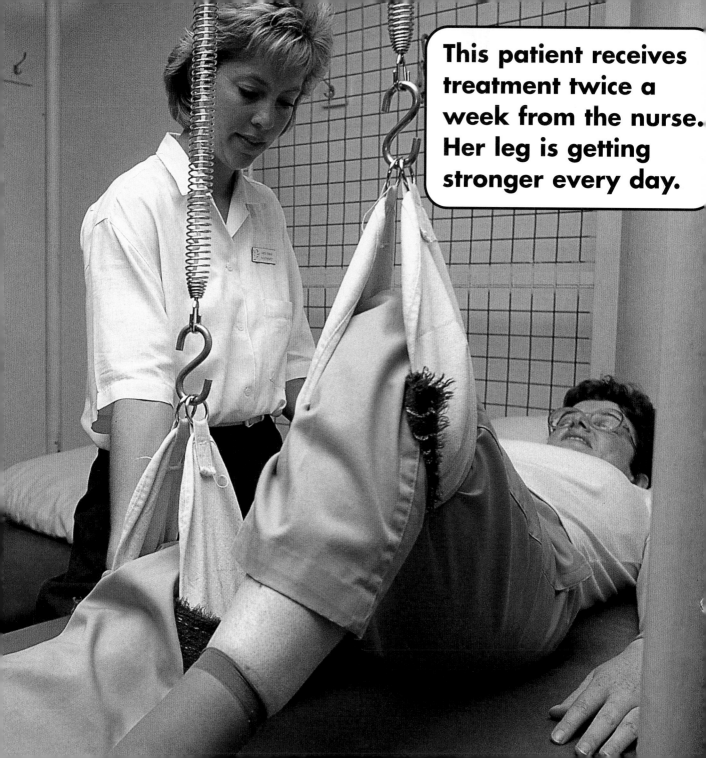